HILARIOUS JOKES

FOR

YEAR OLD KIDS

A Message From the Publisher

Hello! My name is Hayden and I am the owner of Hayden Fox Publishing, the publishing house that brought you this title.

My hope is that you and your young comedian love this book and enjoy every single page. If you do, please think about **giving us your honest feedback via a review on Amazon**. It may only take a moment, but it really does mean the world for small businesses like mine.

Even if you happen to not like this title, please let us know the reason in your review so that we may improve this title for the future and serve you better.

The mission of Hayden Fox is to create premium content for children that will help them increase their confidence and grow their imaginations while having tons of fun along the way.

Without you, however, this would not be possible, so we sincerely thank you for your purchase and for supporting our company mission.

Sincerely,
Hayden Fox

Why should you never trust a pig with a secret?

Because it's bound to squeal.

What do piglets use when they have a rash?

Oinkment

--⁝ DID YOU KNOW? ⁝--

As well as having unique fingerprints, we all have unique tongue prints.

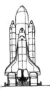

The sun looks super close but it would take about 200 days in our fastest spaceship to reach it.

There is a place where Friday comes before Thursday. Where is it?

In the dictionary.

Before you get into bed, what is the last thing you take off?

You take your feet off the floor.

Seventy seven benevolent elephants

TONGUE TWISTER

Eleven benevolent elephants

Who's there?
A little old lady you.
A little old lady you who?
I didn't know you could yodel!

Knock Knock!

What did one horse say to the other?

You mustang-o with me.

What did one elevator say to the other elevator?

I think I'm coming down with something!

⌁ DID YOU KNOW? ⌁

More than 1 billion people have played Monopoly.

 Every step you take uses 200 different muscles in the body.

Three short sword sheaths.

?

Which five-letter word becomes shorter once two letters are added on?

RIDDLES

„Short."

People climb me, cut me, and burn me; they show me no respect! My rings are not of gold, but they do tell me age.

A tree.

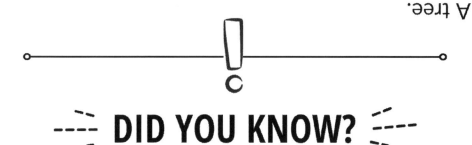

⫶⫶ DID YOU KNOW? ⫶⫶

A prawn or shrimp's heart is in its head.

 A jar of Nutella is sold every 2.5 seconds.

Where do polar bears vote?

The North Poll

Where does Christmas come before Easter?

In the dictionary

Who's there?

Cash.

Cash who?

No thanks, but I'll take a peanut if you have one!

Knock Knock!

RIDDLES

I have keys but no locks. I have space but no room. You can enter, but you can't go outside. What am I?

Keyboard.

In a one-story pink house, there was a pink computer, a pink chair, a pink table, a pink telephone, a pink shower— everything is pink! What color are the stairs here?

There aren't any stairs because it's a one-story house!

Why are cats not good storytellers?

Because they only have 1 tail!

Who's there?

Canoe.

Canoe who?

Canoe come out and play with me?

Why did the pony get sent to his room?

He wouldn't stop horsing around.

What do you call a belt with a clock on it?

A waist of time.

--- DID YOU KNOW? ---

French fries originated in Belgium, not France.

Emperor penguins can last 27 minutes underwater and can dive as deep as 500m.

**Who's there?**
Needle.
Needle who?
Needle little help getting in the door.

**Truly rural,
truly rural,
truly rural,
truly rural...**

Why was the bed wearing a disguise?

Because it was under cover.

When you cross a computer and a life guard...

...You get a screensaver!

What did the llama say before leaving?

Alpaca my bags!

DID YOU KNOW?

Venus and Uranus spin clockwise. They're the only planets that do!

 The footprints on the moon will be there for 100 million years.

Name three consecutive days of the week without using Monday, Tuesday, Wednesday, Thursday, or Friday.

Yesterday, today, and tomorrow.

Timmy throws a ball as hard as he can, and even though no one touches it, it comes back to him. How is this possible?

He throws it up.

I stood sadly on the silver steps of Burgess's fish sauce shop.

Knock Knock!

Who's there?

Boo.

Boo who?

Please don't cry. It's only a joke.

Someone stole my mood ring.

I'm not sure how I feel about that.

Why was the sun suspicious of the umbrella?

It was a little shady.

 **DID YOU KNOW?**

 The world's oldest tree is a pine tree located in California's White Mountain range.
It is over 5,000 years old!

Why was the music teacher good at baseball?

She had the perfect pitch.

What do you call a 100-year-old ant?

ANT-ique.

Who's there?

Candice.

Candice who?

Candice joke get any funnier?

Knock Knock!

Who's there?

Dewey.

Dewey who?

Dewey have to do these jokes all night?

Knock Knock!

What kind of mail does a superstar vampire get?

RIDDLES

Fang mail.

Why was the coach mad?

Because he wanted his quarterback.

DID YOU KNOW?

Babies can't taste salt until they are 4 months old.

The coldest temperature ever recorded on the ground was in Antarctica in 1983. The measurement showed −89.2 °C (−128.6 °F).

Even without being called, they come out at night. However, without being stolen, they are lost during the day. What are they?

Stars.

Why did the mattress go the doctor?

It had spring fever.

TONGUE TWISTER

When I was in Arkansas I saw a saw that could outsaw any other saw I ever saw.

Knock Knock!

Who's there?
Isaac.
Isaac who?
Isaac of knock-knock jokes!

Rhys watched Ross switch his Irish wristwatch for a Swiss wristwatch.

Knock Knock!

Who's there?
Lettuce!
Lettuce who?
Lettuce please stop telling these jokes!

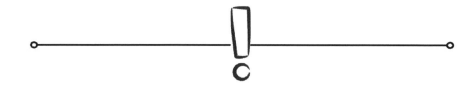

DID YOU KNOW?

Chameleons can change colors in response to changes in temperature, environment, and even mood!

What is taken from the mine, enclosed in a wooden case, and used by everyone despite never being released?

Pencil lead.

Throw away the outside and cook the inside. Then, eat the outside and throw away the inside. What is it?

Corn on the cob.

 Where are chicks born?

In Chick-cago.

Why can't fleas get cold?

They are in fur coats!

What did the croissant say to the knife?

Don't try to butter me up!

What should you give to a sick lemon?

Lemon aid

Why did the picture go to jail?

Because it was framed.

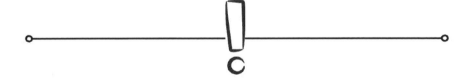

 **DID YOU KNOW?**

An elephant can be pregnant up to 22 months.

Remove my skin and I won't cry, but you might! What am I?

An onion.

You can keep it only after giving it away. What is it?

Your word.

How much caramel can a canny canonball cram in a camel if a canny cannonball can cram caramel in a camel?

TONGUE TWISTER

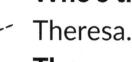

Knock Knock!

Who's there?

Theresa.

Theresa who?

Theresa fly in my soup!

What do dentures and stars have in common?

They both come out at night!

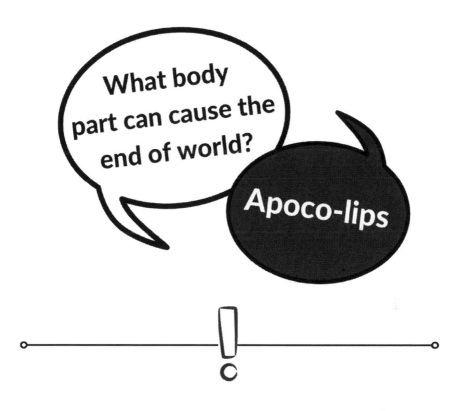

What body part can cause the end of world?

Apoco-lips

--- DID YOU KNOW? ---

The Hawaiian state fish is called a Humuhumunukunukuapua'a. You can also call it a reef triggerfish.

RIDDLES

The more you remove, the larger it grows. What is it?

A hole.

It loses its head in the morning but gets it back in the night. What is it?

A pillow.

Scissors sizzle, thistles sizzle.

TONGUE TWISTER

This is the sixth zebra snoozing thoroughly.

Knock Knock!

Who's there?

Senior.

Senior who?

Senior dog digging in the trash yesterday!

When you look for something, why is it always in the last place you look?

Because when you find it, you stop looking.

What time is it when the clock strikes 13?

Time to get a new clock.

Who's there?
Doctor.
Doctor who?
He's on television.

Who's there?
Gillette.
Gillette who?
If Gillette me in, I won't knock anymore.

⚡ DID YOU KNOW? ⚡

Facial expressions are one of the ways that horses communicate with each other.

 Sea lions can dance to a beat.

If you're keen on stunning kites and cunning stunts, buy a cunning stunning stunt kite.

TONGUE TWISTER

🙂

Who's there?

Alex.

Alex who?

Alexplain everything once you've opened the door.

Knock Knock!

What do you call a boomerang that won't come back?

A stick.

DID YOU KNOW?

The little jump guinea pigs do when they're happy is called popcorning.

Suzie Seaword's fish-sauce shop sells unsifted thistles for thistle-sifters to sift.

A synonym for cinnamon is a cinnamon synonym.

Who's there?

Alfredo.

Alfredo who?

Alfredo the dark!

Please open the door!

Why did the kid bring a ladder to school?

Because she wanted to go to high school.

Where do vampires keep their money?

A blood bank.

DID YOU KNOW?

Bread was invented in Egypt
around 8,000 BC.

Cross cow across a
crowded cow crossing.

Knock Knock!

Who's there?

Alma.

Alma who?

Alma-ny knock-knock jokes can you take?

Why couldn't the pony sing a lullaby?

She was a little hoarse.

What's the smartest insect?

A spelling bee!

Who's there?
Dozen.
Dozen who?
Dozen it get boring answering the door all the time?

DID YOU KNOW?

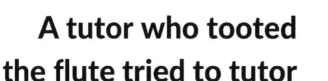

The oldest-known living land animal is a tortoise named Jonathan, who is 187 years old.

A tutor who tooted the flute tried to tutor two tooters to toot.

TONGUE TWISTER

Knock Knock!

Who's there?

Earl.

Earl who?

Earl be glad to tell you if you open the door.

Why didn't the orange win the race?

It ran out of juice.

Why couldn't the astronaut book a hotel on the moon?

Because it was full.

Who's there?
Faraday.
Faraday who?
Faraday last time, open up!

Who's there?
Omar.
Omar who?
Omar goodness gracious, I've got the wrong door!

DID YOU KNOW?

When people go into outer space, their  bodies stretch. Astronauts come back from space a couple of inches taller than when they left.

I thought a thought but the thought I thought wasn't the thought you thought I thought.

TONGUE TWISTER

Knock Knock!

Who's there?
Annabel.
Annabel who?
Annabel would be useful on this door.

What do you call a sleeping bull?

A bulldozer!

Why did the tomato blush?

It saw the salad dressing.

How does a hurricane see?

With one eye.

What do you call a hammock teasing another hammock?

Hammockery!

If one doctor doctors another doctor, then which doctor is doctoring the doctored doctor?

TONGUE TWISTER

Knock Knock!

Who's there?
Belladonna.
Belladonna who?
Belladonna work,
so I had to knock.

 **Why was the man mad at the clock?**

He was ticked off!

Why don't scientists trust atoms?

Because they make up everything!

DID YOU KNOW?

The Amazon rainforest has over 2000 species of butterflies alone.

The human brain is the most complicated thing we have discovered yet.

Lesser leather never weathered wetter weather better.

TONGUE TWISTER

Knock Knock!

Who's there?
Nobel.
Nobel who?
No bell so I'll knock.

 **Why are strawberries natural musicians?**

They love to jam.

Why was the weightlifter upset?

She worked with dumbbells.

What did the policeman say to his tummy?

"Freeze. You're under a vest."

The sixth sick sheik's sixth sheep's sick.

TONGUE TWISTER

Knock Knock!

Who's there?
Ivana.
Ivana who?
Ivana go home.

What's Thanos' favorite app to talk to friends?

Snapchat.

DID YOU KNOW?

The Sahara Desert covers roughly 3.6 million square miles.

A quick witted cricket critic.

Who's there?

Fozzie.

Fozzie who?

Fozzie hundredth time, let me in!

Knock Knock!

How do billboards talk?

Sign language.

What do you call it when your nose is stuffy at the rodeo?

Cowboy Boogie.

Who's there?
Olivia.
Olivia who?
Olivia but I lost the key.

⚆ DID YOU KNOW? ⚆

As of 2015, there are nearly 38 million people living in Tokyo, Japan, ranking it as the most populated city in the world.

Miss Smith's fish-sauce shop seldom sells shellfish.

TONGUE TWISTER

Knock Knock!

Who's there?

Thistle.

Thistle who?

Thistle be the last time I knock on this door!

Did you hear the joke about the roof?

Never mind, it's over your head.

Why are penguins socially awkward?

Because they can't break the ice.

Who's there?

Knock Knock! Egg.

Egg who?

Eggcited to meet you.

Who's there?

Knock Knock! Jamaica.

Jamaica who?

Jamaica lunch for me yet?

--⁝ DID YOU KNOW? ⁝--

There is no atmosphere in space, which means  there is no way for sound to travel and/or be heard. In other words: space is completely silent.

Knock Knock!

Who's there?
Alligator.
Alligator who?
Alligator for her birthday was a card.

Extinct insects' instincts

TONGUE TWISTER

What did the broccoli say to the celery?

"Quit stalking me."

Why are spiders great web developers?

They like finding bugs.

Who's there?
Razor.
Razor who?
Razor hands and dance the boogie!

Who's there?
Rida
Rida who?
Rida lot of books!

DID YOU KNOW?

There's a theory that Earth was struck by a giant object and the collision caused a piece of the Earth to break away, thus creating the moon.

Who's there?

Weevil

Weevil who?

Weevil weevil rock you.

Knock Knock!

Six twin steel steam cruisers.

TONGUE TWISTER

Which superhero hits home runs?

Batman!

Have you heard the rumor about butter?

Never mind, I shouldn't be spreading it.

--⫶ DID YOU KNOW? ⫶--

Despite being the largest animal to have ever lived on planet Earth, the Blue Whale is known to feed on some of the smallest marine animals: tiny shrimp called krill!

Who's there?

Knock Knock! Amos.

Amos who?

A mosquito bit me!

There was a young man called Fisher who was fishing for fish in a fissure.

TONGUE TWISTER

What did the guitar say to the lead singer of the band?

"Stop stringing me along."

Why is a flock of geese like Wikipedia?

They're flying in-formation.

Who's there?

Alpaca.

Alpaca who?

Alpaca the suitcase,
you load up the car!

Knock Knock!

Who's there?

Giraffe.

Giraffe who?

Giraffe anything to eat?
I'm starving!

Knock Knock!

Moses supposes his
toeses are roses.

TONGUE TWISTER

Why is it OK if you forget how to make a boomerang on Instagram?

It will come back to you.

Why did the ghost starch his sheet?

He wanted everyone to be scared stiff.

Who's there?

Gorilla.

Gorilla who?

Gorilla burger, I've got the buns and the relish!

Knock Knock!

Who's there?
Janet.
Janet who?
Janet a big fish?

Knock Knock!

Who's there?
Thumping.
Thumping who?
Thumping green and slimy is climbing up your back!

Preshrunk silk shirts

Who in the solar system has the most loose change?

The moon. It keeps changing quarters.

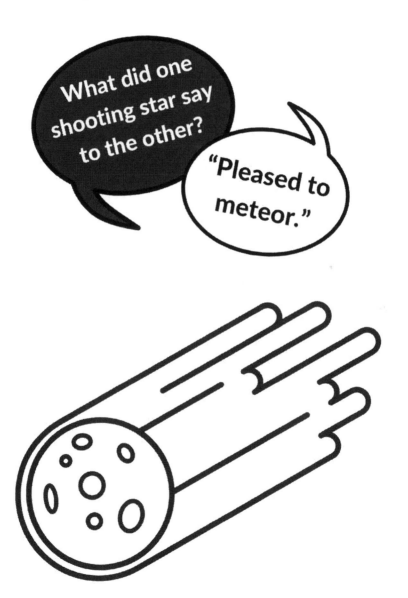

Who's there?

Toucan.

Toucan who?

Toucan play at this game!

Knock Knock!

Who's there?

Cass.

Cass who?

Cass more flies with honey than vinegar!

Knock Knock!

The little red lorry went down Limuru road.

TONGUE TWISTER

The chief of the Leith police dismisses us.

How do you keep an elephant from charging?

Take away her credit card!

How does NASA organize a party?

They planet.

Who's there?

Barbie.

Barbie who?

Barbie-qued chicken is ready if you want some!

 **Knock Knock!**

Who's there?

Beezer.

Beezer who?

Beezer good at making honey.

Knock Knock!

Fred Threlfall's thirty-five fine threads are finer threads than Fred Threlfall's thirty-five thick threads.

TONGUE TWISTER

My teachers told me I'd never amount to much because I procrastinate so much.

I told them, "Just you wait!"

Knock Knock!

Who's there?
Bison.
Bison who?
Bison girl scout cookies!

Knock Knock!

Who's there?
Geno.
Geno who?
Geno I don't like to eat broccoli!

The thistle sifter has a sieve of unsifted thistles she sifts into the sieve of sifted thistles.

What do you say to Simba when he's moving too slow?

Mufasa!

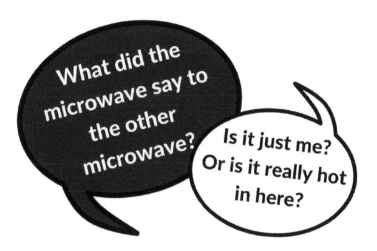

Who's there?

Hammond.

Hammond who?

Hammond eggs for breakfast please!

Who's there?

Oswald.

Oswald who?

Oswald my bubble gum.

Ripe white wheat reapers reap ripe white wheat right.

TONGUE TWISTER

What kind of math do birds love?

Owl-gebra!

What do you call a cow on a trampoline!

A milk shake.

Knock Knock!

Who's there?

Pecan.

Pecan who?

Pecan somebody your own size!

Who's there?
Hubie.
Hubie who?
Hubie-ginning to understand how these jokes work?

Knock Knock!

Who's there?
Argue.
Argue who?
Argue going to let me in?

Knock Knock!

Roberta ran rings around the Roman ruins.

TONGUE TWISTER

Why did the pillow cross the road?

It was picking up the chicken's feathers.

Why haven't you learned the alphabet?

I don't know why (y)!

Mary has seven daughters, and each of them has a brother. Can you figure out the total number of kids Mary has?

Eight; the sisters all have the same brother.

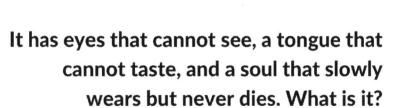

RIDDLES

It has eyes that cannot see, a tongue that cannot taste, and a soul that slowly wears but never dies. What is it?

A shoe.

Who's there?

Major.

Major who?

Major day with this joke!

Knock Knock!

Who's there?

Juliet.

Juliet who?

Will Juliet me in, please?

Knock Knock!

There those thousand thinkers were thinking how did the other three thieves go through.

TONGUE TWISTER

What kind of shoes do ninjas wear?

Sneakers!

What did the mom tomato say to the baby tomato?

C'mon, ketchup!

What is so delicate that it breaks when you say its name?

Silence

RIDDLES

What has a head and a tail but no body?

A coin.

Who's there?
Diana.
Diana who?
Diana thirst too!

Knock Knock!

Who's there?
Stopwatch.
Stopwatch who?
Stopwatcha doin' and open the stupid door.

Knock Knock!

Elizabeth's birthday is on the third Thursday of this month.

TONGUE TWISTER

Six sleek swans swam swiftly southwards

Why can't you tell a joke while ice skating?

Because the ice might crack up!

How did the pirate get his flag so cheap?

He bought it on sail.

I speak without a mouth and hear without ears. I have no-body, but I come alive with the wind. What am I?

An echo!

RIDDLES

What can you catch but not throw?

A cold.

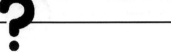

RIDDLES

What goes up but never comes back down?

Your age.

A word I know, six letters it contains, remove one letter and 12 remains, what is it?

Dozens.

Ann's and Andy's anniversary's in April.

TONGUE TWISTER

Knock Knock!

Who's there?
Fido.
Fido who?
Fido known you were home, I'd have brought a cake.

Why did the zombie skip school?

He was feeling rotten.

What treat is never on time?

Choco-late

?

I am an odd number. Take away a letter and I become even. What number am I?

RIDDLES

Seven.

Where can you find cities, towns, shops and streets but no people?

A map.

Who's there?

Pencil

Pencil who?

Pencil fall down if you don't wear a belt.

Knock Knock!

How did the french fry propose to the hamburger?

He gave her an onion ring.

Four furious friends fought for the phone.

TONGUE TWISTER

I wish to wash my Irish wristwatch.

What did the envelope say to the stamp?

Stick with me! We'll go places!

Ten cows and two goats, what would you have?

Plenty of milk.

?

What goes up and down the stairs without moving?

Carpet.

RIDDLES

David's father has three sons: Snap, Crackle, and...?

David.

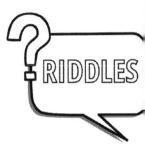

What is always in front of us but can't be seen?

The future.

I am always running, but never get tired or hot. What am I?

A refrigerator/freezer.

Who's there?
Carrie
Carrie who?
Carrie the bags in will you?

 Knock Knock!

On a lazy laser raiser lies a laser ray eraser.

 TONGUE TWISTER

Why do ducks make great detectives?

They always quack the case.

What animal carries an umbrella around?

A reindeer!

What did the taco say to the burrito?

Where you bean?

I sound like I could cut you, but I'm actually quite comfortable. I can be green or yellow. I can be stiff or soft. I am a friend to bugs and also bare feet. What am I?

A blade of grass.

RIDDLES

It's good to stretch me and push my limits. The more you use me, the stronger I get. When I am sharp, I'm at my best. What am I?

A brain.

Knock Knock!

Who's there?
Matthew
Matthew who?
Matthew lace has come
undone!

Knock Knock!

Who's there?
Broken pencil
Broken pencil who?
Oh, never mind it's
pointless!

**Roofs of mushrooms
rarely mush too much.**

What song do vampires hate?

You are my sunshine!

What is an alien's favorite place on a computer?

The space bar!

If you take away one hand, some will remain. What am I?

Handsome.

RIDDLES

A doctor drops off a young boy at school every morning before work. The doctor is not the child's father, but the child is the doctor's son. How is this possible?

The doctor is the child's mom.

Knock Knock!

Who's there?

Doorbell

Doorbell who?

Doorbell delivery!

Knock Knock!

Who's there?

For

For who?

For the hundredth time, it's me!

Sounding by sound is a sound method of sounding sounds.

TONGUE TWISTER

Willie's really weary.

Who's there?
Silence
Silence who?
(Stay quiet)

Who's there?
Water.
Water who?
Water you doing telling jokes right now? Don't you have things to do?

A slimy snake slithered down the sandy Sahara.

TONGUE TWISTER

I wish you were a fish in my dish.

What is brown, hairy and wears sunglasses?

A coconut on vacation.

How do you stop an astronaut's baby from crying?

You rocket!

Seven months have 31 days. How many months have 28 days?

All twelve of them.

What's bright orange with green on top and sounds like a parrot?

A carrot.

Who's there?

Mustache.

Mustache who?

I mustache you a question.

Knock Knock!

Who's there?

Kirtch.

Kirtch who?

God bless you!

Knock Knock!

Rudder valve reversals, rudder valve reversals, rudder valve reversals...

TONGUE TWISTER

Why do ducks always pay with cash?

They always have bills!

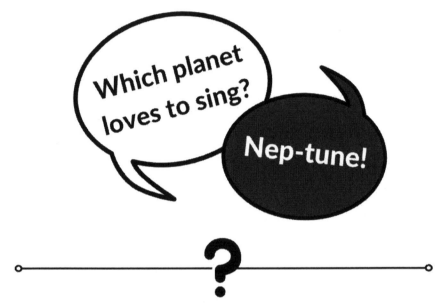

Which planet loves to sing?

Nep-tune!

A girl fell off a 20-foot ladder but she wasn't hurt. How?

She fell off the bottom step

RIDDLES

What has lots of eyes but can't see?

A potato.

Who's there?
Two knee
Two knee who?
Two-knee fish!

Who's there?
Aida.
Aida who?
Aida sandwich for lunch today.

If coloured caterpillars could change their colours constantly could they keep their coloured coat coloured properly?

What's worse than finding a worm in your apple?

Finding half a worm.

Why can't Elsa have a balloon?

Because she will let it go.

I am often following you and copying your every move. Yet you can never touch me or catch me. What am I?

Your shadow.

RIDDLES

How many bricks does it take to complete a brick building?

One brick.

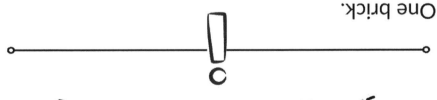

-- DID YOU KNOW? ---

The Nobel Peace Prize is named after Alfred Nobel, the inventor of dynamite.

Who's there?

Alfie.

Alfie who?

Alfie terrible if you don't let me in!

Knock Knock!

Who's there?

Avenue

Avenue who?

Avenue heard this joke before?

Knock Knock!

I saw a kitten eating chicken in the kitchen.

TONGUE TWISTER

Six sticky skeletons.

How do you make an octopus laugh?

With ten-tickles!

What do you call a fake noodle?

An impasta.

-=- DID YOU KNOW? =--

 Ben Franklin only received 2 years of formal education.

Cats are not able to taste anything that is sweet.

Betty's big bunny bobbled by the blueberry bush.

I looked right at Larry's rally and left in a hurry.

Knock Knock!

Who's there?
Dwayne.
Dwayne who?
Dwayne the tub, I'm dwowning.

Knock Knock!

Who's there?
Iona.
Iona who?
Iona new toy!

How do you fix a cracked pumpkin?

With a pumpkin patch.

What do you call a funny mountain?

Hill-arious.

Who keeps the ocean clean?

The mer-maid.

--> DID YOU KNOW? <--

The shortest war in history lasted for only 38 minutes.

DID YOU KNOW?

A male platypus has venom on its hind foot that has enough poison to kill a medium-sized dog.

Knock Knock!

Who's there?

Arfur.

Arfur who?

Arfur got!

Knock Knock!

Who's there?

Iva.

Iva who?

I've a sore hand from knocking!

Why did Johnny throw the clock out of the window?

Because he wanted to see time fly.

What kind of keys are sweet?

Cookies!

DID YOU KNOW?

Kangaroos can not walk backwards.

Hippopotamus milk is pink.

Kindly kittens knitting mittens keep kazooing in the king's kitchen.

I saw Susie sitting in a shoeshine shop.

Who's there?

Vanessa.

Knock Knock!

Vanessa who?

Vanessa time I'll ring the bell!

Who's there?

Olga.

Knock Knock!

Olga who?

Olga home if you don't open up.

What do you call cheese that belongs to someone else?

Nacho cheese!

Why didn't the robot finish his breakfast?

Because the orange juice told him to concentrate.

Where do sheep go on vacation?

The Baaa-hamas.

⋮ DID YOU KNOW? ⋮

Are you terrified that a duck is watching you?

That's known as anatidaephobia.

How can a clam cram in a clean cream can?

Who's there?
King Tut.
King Tut who?
King Tut-key fried chicken!

Who's there?
Woo.
Woo who?
No need to get so excited; it's just a joke!

What did the traffic light say to the truck?

Don't look, I'm changing.

Who was that owl who did all the tricks?

Who-dini.

What kind of vegetable is angry?

A steamed carrot!

?

What has hands, but can't clap?

A clock.

RIDDLES

I look at you, you look at me, I raise my right, you raise your left. What am I?

Your reflection in a mirror.

What do you call a deer with no eyes?

"No eye-deer."

 What did the mouse say to the keyboard?

You're my type!

Who's there?
Larva.
Larva who?
I larva you!

Who's there?
Honey bee.
Honey bee who?
Honey bee a sweetie and get me some water.

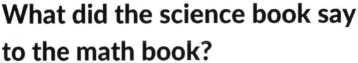

What did the science book say to the math book?

Wow, you've got problems.

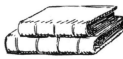

How do squids get to school?

They take an octobus.

Where do mermaids look for jobs?

The kelp-wanted section.

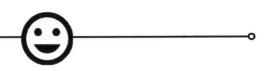

Knock Knock!

Who's there?

Patsy.

Patsy who?

Patsy dog on the head, he likes it.

She sold six shabby
sheared sheep on ship.

A bloke's back
brake-block broke.

I run along your property and
all around the backyard, yet I
never move. What am I?

A fence.

If two is company and three is a crowd,
what are four and five equal to?

Nine.

Why do scissors always win a race?

Because they take a shortcut!

Where does a rat go when it has a toothache?

To the rodentist.

Why didn't the hyena cross the road?

He was too busy laughing.

 Why did the chicken go the hospital?

Because it needed some tweatment!

--- **DID YOU KNOW?** ---

Goats have rectangular pupils in their eyes rather than circular ones.

Elizabeth has eleven elves in her elm tree.

Craig Quinn's quick trip to Crabtree Creek.

Knock Knock!

Who's there?
Tank.
Tank who?
You're welcome!

Knock Knock!

Who's there?
Anita?
Anita who?
Anita borrow a pencil!

Why did the dragon cross the road?

Because he was too chicken to fly!

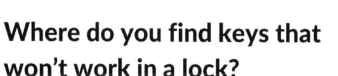

Where do you find keys that won't work in a lock?

RIDDLES

On a piano.

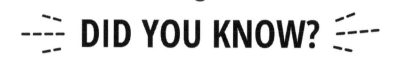

‑‑‑ DID YOU KNOW? ‑‑‑

There are 31,556,926 seconds in a year.

Cans of diet soda will float in water but regular soda cans will sink.

A tsunami can travel as fast as a jet plane.

Who's there?

Possum.

Possum who?

Possum gravy on my potatoes.

Knock Knock!

What is a vampire's favorite fruit?

A blood orange!

Why did the phone walk in the water?

He was wading for a phone call.

❄ How do you find Will Smith in the snow?

You look for fresh prints.

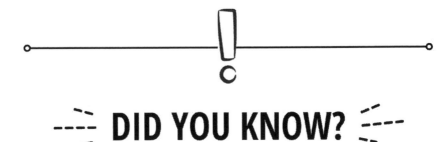

⸝⸝ DID YOU KNOW? ⸝⸝

Your hair and nails are made of keratin, which is found in beaks, hooves, horns, porcupine quills and turtle shells.

Which state is the smartest?

Alabama—it has four As and one B!

What do attorneys wear to court?

Law-suits!

DID YOU KNOW?

Bulls are actually colorblind and so they can't see the color red.

Before trees existed, giant white mushrooms covered most of the Earth's land.

Leave Your Feedback on Amazon

Please think about leaving some feedback via a review on Amazon. It may only take a moment, but it really does mean the world for small businesses like mine.

Even if you did not enjoy this title, please let us know the reason(s) in your review so that we may improve this title and serve you better.

From the Publisher

Hayden Fox's mission is to create premium content for children that will help them expand their vocabulary, grow their imaginations, gain confidence, and share tons of laughs along the way.

Without you, however, this would not be possible, so we sincerely thank you for your purchase and for supporting our company mission.

Check out our other books!

For more, visit our Amazon store at:
amazon.com/author/haydenfox

Made in United States
Orlando, FL
30 October 2021